BETWEEN YOU AND ME

BY

CYNTHIA GODIN

Published by:
A Snowy Day Distribution & Publishing
P.O. Box 2014
Merrimack, NH 03054
(603) 493-2276

First Edition

ISBN: 978-1-936615-37-7
Printed in the United States of America

Also available as an ebook.
ISBN: 978-1-936615-38-4

This book is dedicated to my entire family. You are the reason I am the person I am today. The reason I love so hard and feel so deeply. You are in my every thought, every moment of every day. You are my everything.

"There is a time for everything.
And whatever you are doing
right now that is the time for that.

So be present in that moment.
Don't be in a different time.

Don't be ruminating on the past
or worrying about the future.

Don't live in guilt, regret, or shame.

Don't live with worry, fear, and
apprehension.

Live in the moment.
The time is right now.

There is a time for everything.

And when it's that time be
there and nowhere else."

Dr. Richard Beck

Come take my hand,
And walk with me.

Take me in your arms,
And dance with me.

Hold me forever,
And open up your heart.

Love me forever.

YOUTH

"Youth above all is a collection of possibilities."
Albert Camus

Between you and me, you never realize how wonderful your childhood is until you are an adult. Youth is truly wasted on the young as the old saying goes.

Childhood is innocent. It is a time of discovery and make-believe. It is a time when there is no focus on days, weeks, months, or years. A truly magical time when each waking moment is spent doing all the things that truly make you happy.

The time you spend with your friends, daydreaming and

fantasizing about how life will be someday is truly wasted. Life is never what you dream. Life is full of reality, heartache, and worry. Life is all about being a grown up, working, paying bills, and hoping to meet that special someone someday.

What we need to do is return to that state of innocence. That instant when nothing makes you happier than living in the moment. Forget about the housework. It will wait another day. Live, breathe, inhale, imagine, live in the moment.

We are so trained to the day to day and week to week schedule that before we know it the weeks are gone! Ever wonder why as a child time seemed to go so slow but as an adult time flies by? As a child there is no emphasis on time. As adults time is passing us by in the blink of an eye. We need to slow down.

Okay so this is coming from a person who much of the time worked 60 to 70 hours a week. I worried about money. I worried about making ends meet. About what bill was due next week. Many nights I lay awake thinking about what needed to be done and would actually set off a panic attack! So I worked, and worked, and worked...until I got laid off.

So okay I worked my butt off. Lived day to day. Worried every minute. Kept myself awake at night wondering how to make it, and guess what? I am laid off making ends meet anyway! Sure I have all the same worries but I have me time. Time I did not give myself before. So this got me thinking...what good is

3

working like a dog and not enjoying myself if I am going to be in the same boat anyway?!

If we can find a happy medium life would be so much sweeter. I think about when I was a child; four children went to school while two parents worked. When the weekend came things needed to get done around the house but there also needed to be some play time. My parents had one day of our weekend spent cleaning the house. The other day we went to Magic Mountain, San Juan Capistrano, the beach, wherever. Family time, out of the house, laughing and bonding. What a reward for a long week for all! That is the way life should be. What good is working hard all your life saving and getting by not to get the chance to enjoy it as you go?

*Somewhere childhood memories
lie in solitude,*

*Locked frozen faraway,
sleeping,*

*Somehow waiting to be
unleashed.*

SELF-ACCEPTANCE

"Often it is not about becoming
a new person, but becoming
the person you were meant
to be and already are but
don't know how to be."

Heath Buckaster

Between you and me, if you truly
want to be happy you need to learn
to accept yourself for who you are.
How do you expect others to love
you if you can't even love yourself?

We all have our quirks. For some of
us it is weight. For others it may be
that our hair is thinning or our nose
is too big. Who cares? Look around,
nobody is really perfect. You need to

love who you are for every little flaw there is because that is what makes you special.

We really are amazing. We come into this world unable to function for ourselves and turn into amazing beings able to do virtually anything. Our bodies have the ability to heal and create life. We really are special and we need to start realizing that.

I once lost 100 pounds. I felt like a million bucks! But you know what? The only person that really cared anything about the 100 pound weight loss was me. My family still loved me the same. My friends still looked at me the same way. Nothing really changed at all. I was still the same me.

Sure there are things we can do to make sure we live a longer healthier life but we need to stop trying to be something we are not. If others cannot accept us for all of our imperfections, they do not deserve a place in our life.

What we need to do is focus on our strengths. Be proud of who we are and where we have come. Love ourselves for what we are. Radiate confidence and you will attract positive people in your life who appreciate you and love you for everything you are. Surround yourself with people like this and you will soon forget the negative.

When the whole world seems to
get you down,

Turn that frown upside down.

Take a moment, step back, and
look around.

You'll find life's really not that
bad,

There no reason to get upset
and mad.

Refocus, regroup, and move
along.

Simply remember all your hopes
and dreams.

You can be anything you want
to be.

Don't let fear and uncertainty
take that away.

It's up to you, to prove
everyone wrong.

It's up to you, to take the
changes that come along.

It's up to you, to be the best you
can be.

It's up to you.

We all need to learn to laugh at
ourselves,

Especially those of us who look
like elves.

Gee you don't seem that bad at
all.

The next time someone makes
you sad.

Imagine them with a big nose
and red clown hair.

Suddenly things won't seem so bad at all.

So remember all your hopes and dreams.

You can be anything you want to be.

Don't let fear and uncertainly take that right away.

It's up to you, to prove everyone wrong.

It's up to you, to take chances that come along.

It's up to you, to be the best you can be.

It's up to you.

FAMILY

"Family is the most important thing in the world."

Princess Diana

Between you and me, family is everything. Without family there is nothing. There is no love, no meaning, no reason.

As a youth we spend every minute with our family. But somewhere along the line, as teenagers, we prefer our friends to our family. Family time becomes less and less until the day we leave home and see our family only on a few occasions.

Family should be the most important thing in your life! It is all about family. Family that raises you.

13

Family you play with. And
eventually the new family you
marry and create. Family is
everything. Family truly should be
everything.

People have always asked why my
family sees each other so much?
Why do we celebrate every birthday
and special occasion together?
Family is everything. You could
have all the money in the world but
if you do not have family to love and
hold and care for it is a lonely life.

Love one another. See each other.
Listen to each other. You never
know when something will happen
because life can be cruel. Tell each
other how you feel. Every chance
you get! Every phone call should end
with I love you. Every time a family
member leaves it should end with a
kiss or a hug. Don't be that person

who wonders, "What the last thing I said to my dear loved one?"

I lived in Florida for 6 years while my family was in New England. They made it a point to come see us a couple times a year and we made it a point to come back home. We talked on the phone constantly and emailed back and forth. Eventually our second child was born and we realized it was not fair to our children to be so far away and see family only a few times a year. So we made the trek home. My children were able to grow up with grandparents, aunts and uncles, and cousins.

Believe in the power of love. Believe in each other and hold on to each other. You only get one family. Love them every day.

Without you in my life,

Every day is an endless struggle.

With you by my side,

I have the strength to live forever.

LOVE

"I like to believe that love is a reciprocal thing, that it can't really be felt truly by one."

Sean Penn

Between you and me, there is no love greater than friendship. Being best friends is the main ingredient in any love story.

So much focus is put on love. As teens we are stressed, trying to find someone to spend time with so we are not alone. Of course, we cannot be the only one without a boyfriend or girlfriend, right? Wrong!

I have been there and done that. I always had to be with someone. Fear of being alone, I guess. I hooked up with the wrong people just so I would not be alone. Admit it, we all do it. But why? Can you really say that it was worth it half the time?

I met a man who was a wonderful friend. We were both in relationships. The four of us hung out all the time. We became the best of friends. Years later, after relationships ended, he and I became closer and eventually, lovers. Then one lucky day, I married him, my very best friend.

I am telling you: You have to be friends first.

My parents met and had an instant attraction. They became good friends. Forty-nine years later, they are still in love.

Your soul mate WILL be your best friend. Don't rush love. Be best *friends first. Friends who understand each other and share the same interests. Friends who truly enjoy being together and want to be together in everything they do.*

My nephew once told me he hoped to be as lucky in love as we are. What a wonderful thing to hear! I told him, "Stop looking so hard to find love. You will meet someone when you least expect it. You will become close friends and eventually, realize you love this someone; not for looks, but for how this someone makes you feel. When you find your thoughts consumed by this someone and a desire to be with this someone every waking moment of the day, this someone will be 'the one.' This someone will make you feel whole. Most of all, this someone will be your best friend."

Her gaze is that of a star-crossed lover.

His look is laden with desire.

After all these years of marriage.

Their love burns just as strong.

The food of love is still found strong.

GIVE AND TAKE

"If love doesn't know how to give and take without restriction, it is not love, but a transaction that never fails to lay stress on a plus and minus."

Emma Goldman

Between you and me, there is a little give and take in every great relationship.

Any great relationship, be it a friendship or lovers, is based on the understanding that you need to give and take. Being understanding of your partner's needs as much as they understand yours.

I, for instance, love romance. I love to read it. I love to watch it. I love to live by it. My husband, however, loves action and mayhem. As much as he needs to understand he is with a hopeless romantic and allow me to watch romantic comedies, I have to be willing to watch his 'Sons of Anarchy.'

Being able to give and take is a perfect way to show how committed you are to each other. I once knew of a couple that loved going to concerts. Their taste differed. And while she was willing to go with him to see his bands, he refused to go see her bands because he did not like them. No surprise they did not make it six months in their relationship.

Sharing the same interests is great but there is no way you can like all the same things. Be willing to give in sometimes and appreciate your partner's interests. Funny thing is, you just may realize you kinda, sorta, like it too!

Be willing to switch off what movies you see. Take turns choosing what to do when you go out. Appreciate each other for your interests and share with each other.

For our anniversary one year, I spent hundreds of dollars to take my husband to the Battle of the Bays, which was the Tampa Bay Buccaneers versus the Green Bay Packers. You know what? Not only was that one fabulous anniversary gift he has never forgotten, I loved it! I had so much fun and brag about it to this very day!

And I can honestly say that when my parents bought us anniversary tickets one year to see Phantom of the Opera, because that is my absolute favorite opera in the world, he loved it! At the outset, he was very scared, let me tell you. He had never been to an opera before and had his reservations, but he still talks about it to this very day!

Be willing to share in every aspect of each other. It is the greatest way to say not only, "I love you," but also, "I appreciate who you are."

From fragments of a symphony,

A dream was created.

With desire and dreams,

A beautiful melody was created.

FIGHTING

"Fighting fair is about respecting your spouse, even in moments of disagreement."

Desiree S. Coleman

Between you and me, there is no winner in a fight. No one truly walks away a winner in a fight, there are always bruises.

We all know there are logical fighters and there are emotional fighters. Which is better? Who really knows. The trick is to understand what kind of fighters you and your partner are and work together.

I am a logical fighter. I do not yell and scream. I very calmly and most

likely freakishly, quietly point out
what I do not like and what had
better change if he wishes to
continue to inhabit the earth.

My husband is an emotional fighter.
He personally feels persecuted, as if
standing before a firing squad. As a
result he yells and cusses and
basically loses it.

So which is better? Neither really. I
am so full of logic that to hear
otherwise is impossible making me
not a very good listener in an
argument. That is really not fair, I
know. Being so emotional, it is
impossible to hear something logical
and make sense of it.

So what do you do? First, you have
to admit what type of fighter you
are and recognize your faults. Be
more understanding of the type of

fighter your partner is. If he is loud, lower your tone. If she is being unreasonable tell her to stop and listen to your side for a moment.

Whatever you do, do not say things you will regret later. The words you speak out loud in a fight are still truths. They are truths you would never say unless anger had blinded you. But you can never take them back. Remember to be sensitive to the angry words because they just might cause a bruise that can never heal.

I believe it is important to walk away for a few minutes; it is important to have a chance to think about the issue at hand. I know for me, sometimes, I have misunderstood the way something was said or even that part of it may be true. Giving each other a few minutes to calm down puts a lot of the fire out in an argument. You can go back and talk rather than yell and each party is open to listening. So it is okay to say I need a few minutes to think and look at it from your side.

Some people can fight about anything. I say the only way to deal with this is to pick your battles. Not everything needs to be a fight. You need to realize what is important to you and fight for those beliefs. Let the little things slide. We are all entitled to our own opinions even if other people do not agree. Do not fall victim to the person who voices their opinion so regularly that every time they open their mouth you feel the need to say something. You know why? They live for confrontation. They enjoy getting you worked up and seeing what you will do. Forget about it. The only person it really bothers in the end is you.

And most importantly, do not go to bed angry. Resolve your issues and make up before you fall asleep. Not only will they keep you from the rest you need but the feelings will fester and continue the next day.

Thank you for the time you took,
To listen to me as I shook.

For always being by my side,
When I just knew I couldn't make
it even if I tried.

For lighting the way when the
way seemed dark,
Thanks for continuing to light
that dying spark.

I knew I could always rely on you,
You always had the strength to
see things through.

Thanks for never losing hope,
For never hating me for the mean
words I spoke.

You always realized how I needed you there,

I just needed to know someone really did care.

I may never have let you know,

Sometimes it is hard to let your feelings show.

But in time it becomes easier to care,

To let your feelings be known if you dare.

I love you and I hope you know,

I love you and now I can let it show.

MONEY

"Money has never made man happy, nor will it. There is nothing in its nature to provide happiness. The more of it one has the more one wants."

Benjamin Franklin

Between you and me, if you cannot put your money together and think of it as "our money" you can never truly be one.

I know there are multitudes of people out there who believe that her money is hers and his money is his but you know what? Someday, and at some point, it will come back to haunt you.

I once knew a couple who decided that he would pay the mortgage, cable, and electric, while she would pay daycare, groceries, clothes, etc. Eventually, I heard him say, "Sure she pays those things but my bills total $2500 while hers are only $1000."

I have heard of another couple who hold a joint account in which equal money is contributed to cover the bills while each person maintains a separate account. Eventually, I heard, "Sure we put equal amounts into the account to pay the bills, but he makes $2000 more a month than I do and I have no idea where all his money goes."

Face it. If you cannot sit down, put your money together, pay the bills together, both knowing exactly what you have and where the rest is going, you are not one.

Sure even putting all the money together and knowing where it is there will always be fights about money; however, at least you are working together for a common goal. You both will have a better understanding of what you can afford and why some things will have to wait.

Money will always be an issue in any relationship. Understanding that and being able to work together makes it so much easier for you both to know exactly where the money is without any secrets.

Tax return money is house money. No matter who worked and who stayed home with the children, the money belongs to both parties. Either it is put away for a rainy day, spent catching up on bills or *paying something off, or used for family vacations.*

I cannot tell you how frustrating it is to hear, "The tax money is mine because I made more and had more tax money taken out," or "Well, I worked and she stayed home with the kids, so really, it is my money."

As far as I am concerned that is so wrong. No matter who made more money in a relationship, you are equals. You are partners. You have chosen to spend your life together. So sit down and figure out a common way for the money to be spent. And I am sorry but a stay-at-home mother works just as hard cleaning the house, taking care of the children, cooking the meals, etc. Exactly how much money is saved by having her stay home with the children?

Work together. Share together. Save together. Appreciate how hard you worked as a couple to get where you are and have what you have.

We made a promise before all we knew,

Said we would always see it through.

Times got tough and money got tight,

We fought, we struggled, we made it right.

Together we made it, never let the bond sever,

We stood the test of time, together forever.

CHORES

"Chivalry is not just a fancy
word with a neat meaning;
it's a way of life."
Vaughn Ripley

Between you and me, gone are the
days when the women cleaned the
house and the men did the yard
work. Being able to share
responsibilities should be a way of
life when you choose to be together.

I am often shocked how many times
my husband and I go out to do the
yard work and around us only the
men are outside doing the same. I
just could not imagine sending my
husband out to mow the lawn and do
all the yard work himself! I can

honestly say the same thing every winter when we are out shoveling snow and only the men are doing it around the neighborhood.

Why is it acceptable for these women to sit back and watch their husband do these chores by themselves? Is it because he refuses to help with any chores in the house? That is just crazy!

My husband mows the lawn while I weed-whack and/or blow off the porch, etc. If my husband is home when I am cooking, he usually offers to help out.

My husband, my children, and I – all of us - take an active part in cleaning up the kitchen and putting the dishes away. Sometimes I start the laundry, other times he does.

Sharing chores is an excellent way of showing you appreciate each other. I truly believe being able to share these responsibilities makes working together in a marriage so much easier, because you are both willing to work hard – together.

Laughter breaks the silence,
Soft chatter fills the void.

He is chopping onions,
She is stirring the pot.

As she reaches across, her arm
brushes his,
He looks up at her and smiles.

Not a word is needed to break the
silence,
The mood fills the air.

PARENTS

"Love your parents. We are so busy growing up, we often forget they are also growing old."

Unknown

Between you and me, your parents are the reason you exist. Without them there would be no you.

Why is it that our parents raise us, teach us right from wrong, guide us, and support everything that we are and yet so many people forget that? I am so shocked to learn how infrequently people visit their parents or call them. It is just beyond my level of understanding I guess.

Okay sure, there are some pretty horrific situations out there that I completely understand children leaving home and never looking back but really I cannot believe that is largely the case. So why then is it such a chore to spend time with the people who gave you life?

Sure I may be the exception. I live an hour away and for the most part see my parents once a week and talk to them every day by phone or text. But really is it that much to ask to call at least once every couple of days and try to see them every couple of weeks?

I can honestly say to my children, "I will be crushed, broken hearted, and probably seek you out in vengeance if I do not hear from you at least once a week and see you every couple of weeks once you leave home.

For crying out loud I gave you everything you better at least give me that!"

My parents were strict. We were taught what was expected and to have respect. We were given freedom to make our mistakes and learn from them. Sometimes this came with a lecture or guidance in the right direction. We were always supported no matter what our choices even when they knew it was a complete mistake. They held our hand when we cried and cheered on our accomplishments. I harbor no ill will towards any of their choices raising us. They did the best they could for four children. Sure I may not carry on all the same parenting skills as they did but for the large part I tried because whatever else I believe they raised four pretty great kids and it was my biggest hope I would do the same for my two children.

I cannot imagine not having the connection we share. I would never want any other of the relationships I have seen over the years. I love every minute we spend together and simple "Hello" texts we share. My parents are the greatest because they raised me to be who I am and I can only hope my children feel the same way when they leave home someday and eventually raise their own children.

As we sail the ocean of life,

We are surrounded by your love.

You are the hull of our existence, lending us your shell,

As protection from the crashing waves life has thrust upon us.

You are our keel, balancing and stabilizing us from rocking too much,

As you embrace us in your loving grasp.

With you as our rudder, we are steered clear of the rocks,

And set back on course when we sway.

Your tiller gives us strength
when the days seem long,

As you cling to us and never let
go.

Your strong mast is standing
tall and proud,

As you watch over us and
support us in all our decisions.

Just as your boom allows us
extra support,

When we seem to lose sight of
our destination.

Your sail gives us guidance and
power,

Allowing us to flow free
exploring new channels.

With you as our vessel,

We can sail any sea and
weather any storm.

Together we shall always be,

As we sail the endless sea.

CHILDREN

"A child must know that he is a miracle. That since the beginning of the world there hasn't been, and until the end of the world there will never be, another child like him."

Pablo Casals

Between you and me, children are everything. The best thing you ever did in your entire life was create your children.

I once read an obituary from a family who lost their child to drugs. The message was simple: Your children are your everything.

Pay attention. Love them. See them. Be a part of them.

After I read that, I cried my eyes out. I realized I may not have done everything right in my life, but I did a phenomenal job raising my children, and they are the center of my world.

Years ago, it was not like that. Once a child was 18, they were out the door. That does not seem to be the case as much anymore, thank goodness!

Just because your child is over 18 does not mean a magic switch is hit and your child is out of your life. Your children were the center of your world for 18 years, so keep them there forever!

Sure children need their space to grow but call or text them, just to let

them know your thinking of them.
Get together for birthdays. Have
dinner together when you can.
Family is everything.

As a child, I remember doing
everything with my parents. Very
rarely were we left with a
babysitter. Many invitations were
turned down if children were not
invited. I remember that. I
appreciated that.

I chose to carry on in that fashion
with my children. Very rarely did
we leave our children with a
babysitter. We turned down many
invitations that did not include our
children. There will be plenty of time
for that when they leave home was
my belief. I know my children
appreciated that. They loved being a
part of all we did. And as they got
older and had the choice of being

with us, most times they still chose to come with my husband and me.

I feel very strongly about that so I included it as part of my lecture to my children about their future. My long winded lecture consisted of this: Go to school. Get a good job. See the world. Buy your fancy cars and go on your expensive vacations. Eventually buy your house and set down your roots. Get married, have children, and love your life, spending every moment with your children, because you know you have done all the crazy stuff already and you will never regret a moment of it.

We will have to wait and see what the future holds as one of my children is still in college and one in his final years of high school.

I look at you and can't help but smile,

You are everything I wished I could be.

You have the strength needed to cope,

But the tenderness to understand when it is needed.

I watched you grow and am consumed with pride,

How could something so good come of me?

Every day is a precious gift,

I will hold on to these memories forever.

SIBLINGS

"They say that no matter how old you become, when you are with your siblings you revert back to childhood."

Karen White

Between you and me, the relationship you have with your siblings should be special.

As children the relationship between siblings has good times and bad. Sometimes you are very tight and have a great bond. Other times as you each try to make your own way in the world the relationship becomes strained.

In most cases this rocky relationship continues on into adulthood. At

times you are there for each other
and still there are times when it
seems you just don't have time for
each other.

It is very hard not to have jealousies
and resentments develop. We have
to remember we all came from the
same place. We are family good or
bad. The way one sibling chooses to
live may not be the way another
chooses but that is their choice. We
need to respect each other for our
successes and failures.

I have seen brothers that completely
hate each other and have nothing
good to say about each other. When
you truly listen to what they say it is
jealousy. One lives free without a
care for money or possessions while
the other works to "pay the man."
Or two sisters that can't even be in
the same room with each other. But

all they want is to be accepted by the other and not be judged for their choices.

You only get one family. You need to accept each other and not judge. The way you choose to live your life may not be the way I choose to live mine but who says either is right. Life is too short to be jealous and angry. Get over it. Move on. Be a family and love each other.

You played together as children.

Learning to appreciate each other's interests.

Moved aside and let them have the win when they needed it.

Had their back through thick and thin.

Grew up seeing things differently.

Made your way in the world as you saw fit.

Sometimes it's hard to look back and believe how close you were.

You grow up and have new obligations.

Treasure each moment you have,

Life is too short to let it drift away.

TRADITIONS

"Good habits formed at youth make all the difference."

Aristotle

Between you and me, there is no time like the present to start traditions.

Let's face it, some of the things you choose to believe are important eventually your children will think are silly. And you know what? That's okay.

As I have explained to my children, there are things I have done while you were growing up you came to love. Decorating for each holiday. Celebrating Halloween. However, there are things you probably did not like. As punishment you lost something important to you. Getting together for every birthday, holiday, etc. may have been too much for you. That's okay. It is up to you to choose what was and is important to you and carry it on with your family.

I have seen many people who do not decorate for holidays. I have seen families not get together for Thanksgiving or Christmas each year and frankly it breaks my heart. I cannot believe that is how they were raised. I cannot believe that these traditions were not passed down. Where did we go wrong as a society?

So much is changing in the world around us that it is up to us to just say, "Stop!" Sitting on the porch on Sunday used to be something people did. Now you hardly see that anymore. Everyone is too busy.

People used to go for Sunday drives and stop in to visit people. Now you need to make an "appointment" two weeks ahead to be able to get together. Somewhere along the way we forgot the traditions of our ancestors.

Things we love should be shared. Can't we just take a few minutes to reevaluate what is important to us and make it a point to bring it back? Share with our children those things that put a smile on our face when we were children?

Oh the pretty lights I see,

All the decorations on the tree.

Family and friends all gathered around,

Food and laughter abound.

These traditions have taken over me,

How I wish to share with thee.

THE LITTLE THINGS

"Enjoy the little things in life for someday you will look back and realize they were a big thing."

Robert Brault

Between you and me, it is the little things that mean the most. Taking a second to appreciate someone is the best way to say "I love you."

We make it a point to acknowledge people on their birthday and special occasions and that is important, but what happens the rest of the year? Why do we feel there is no need to shower each other with kindness for absolutely no other reason?

Taking a moment to do something special for someone can brighten his or her day. It is an important element to great relationships. I remember when my husband and I first started living together. Each week he cashed his paycheck he would buy me a single rose. It was such a simple thing but it meant the world to me.

When I go shopping and see something my husband or children would like I pick it up. It isn't because they have asked or even because I feel it is necessary. It is simply because I saw it and thought of them.

This applies with anything. I am usually responsible for picking up the house but when someone empties the dishwasher on their own or takes the dog out to me it says, "I appreciate what you do and want to contribute."

If we could all be mindful of each other and surprise each other with little gestures not only will it bring us closer but it can help when someone is having a bad day. There is so much stress in our everyday lives we need a little goodness. A few minutes to feel special.

You don't even realize what
you do to me,

How that simple gesture leaves
my heart pounding.

You can't even begin to
understand,

The way your lingering touch
melts my heart.

You have no idea how your love
affects me,

When you look so deep within
my soul.

You make every moment
special,

You can't even begin to
comprehend.

PUTTING IT ALL TOGETHER

"The true secret of happiness lies in taking a genuine interest in all the details of daily life."

William Morris

Between you and me, we need to learn to take life a little slower. Live, breath, love, and hold on to each other.

From the time we are children, we are trying to wish our life away. "I can't wait to grow up!" How silly that seems now as an adult. If we only knew then what we know now, we would cherish every moment and enjoy life.

As we become teenagers we enter an age where we can't get away with childish things anymore but are not old enough to make our own decisions. "Someday when I am older I will do whatever I want!" What we did not realize then was this was a time of discovery. A time when we could choose our path. If we only had the chance to go back and relax a little. If we could have understood our parents only wanted the best for us and made choices to better ourselves instead of rushing to move out and be on our own.

Instead of rushing love if we could slow it down a little. Avoid so much hurt along the way making the wrong choices. Letting that special person find you and knock your socks off. Make lasting friendships instead of so many people coming in and out of our lives.

Realizing when you find that special someone that any good relationship requires work. You need to learn to work together. Stop fighting all the time. Life is too short. Live in the moment.

Raise our children to love and support them in everything they do. Be together. Play together. Grow together.

Life can be hard but it can be a beautiful thing if you focus on the good. Don't dwell in the past. It is over and done. Start living for today.

Today is the day I start to live.

I have had so much to learn.

I will promise to open my heart.

I will give unselfishly of myself.

I am going to be a better friend.

I will hold you close and comfort you.

I will be a better child, sibling, and lover.

I can accept you for who you are.

I will be there for my children.

I will always be here for you.

Today is the day I will learn to love unconditionally.

Between you and me, life is more than the cars we drive, the money we make, the home we live in, and the crowd we hang with. Life is about love and caring. Not being afraid to love who we are and where we come from.

We need to take a step back, reevaluate, and refocus on what is important in life.

About the Author

Cynthia lives in Massachusetts with her husband of nineteen years and two children.
She enjoys reading, writing poetry, and spending time with her family.

www.ingramcontent.com/pod-product-compliance
Lightning Source LLC
Chambersburg PA
CBHW071420040426
42445CB00012BA/1225